LAUGH-OUT-LOUD JOKES

LAUGH-OUT-LOUD SPACE JOKES

CAITIE MCANENEY

WINDMILL BOOKS

Published in 2025 by Windmill Books, an Imprint of Rosen Publishing
2544 Clinton St., Buffalo, NY 14224

First Edition

Editor: Caitie McAneney
Book Design: Claire Zimmermann

Photo Credits: Cover, p.1 (child) Anatoliy Karlyuk/Shutterstock.com; series art (paper texture) OanaGherghe2/Shutterstock.com; cover, pp. 1 (planets, stars, UFO, and asteroid illustrations), 4, 6, 8, 10, 14 (rocks), 16, 18, 20, 22, 23 Nadzin/Shutterstock.com; cover, pp.1 (satellite illustration), 12, 14 (astronaut) Macrovector/Shutterstock.com; p. 5 LightField Studios/Shutterstock.com; p. 7 Larysa Dubinska/Shutterstock.com; p. 9 Sharomka/Shutterstock.com; p. 11 draganab/iStock; p. 13 Nzoka John/iStock; p. 15 popcorner/Shutterstock.com; p. 17 anatoliy_gleb/iStock; p. 19 Jasonfang/iStock; p. 21 Sotnikova Vera/Shutterstock.com.

Library of Congress Cataloging-in-Publication Data

Names: McAneney, Caitie, author.
Title: Laugh-out-loud space jokes / Caitie McAneney.
Description: Buffalo : Windmill Books, 2025. | Series: Laught-out-loud jokes | Includes index.
Identifiers: LCCN 2024012430 (print) | LCCN 2024012431 (ebook) | ISBN 9781538396957 (library binding) | ISBN 9781538396940 (paperback) | ISBN 9781538396964 (ebook)
Subjects: LCSH: Outer space–Juvenile humor. | Space flight–Juvenile humor. | Wit and humor, Juvenile.
Classification: LCC PN6231.S645 M33 2025 (print) | LCC PN6231.S645 (ebook) | DDC 818/.602–dc23/eng/20240401
LC record available at https://lccn.loc.gov/2024012430
LC ebook record available at https://lccn.loc.gov/2024012431

Manufactured in the United States of America

CPSIA Compliance Information: Batch #CSWM25. For further information, contact Rosen Publishing at 1-800-237-9932

CONTENTS

Words in the glossary appear in **bold** the first time they are used in the text.

GIMME SOME SPACE!

How do you organize a party in space?

YOU PLANET!

What kind of books do planets read?

COMET BOOKS.

Why don't famous people go to the moon?

IT HAS NO ATMOSPHERE.

What was the first animal in space?

THE COW THAT JUMPED OVER THE MOON.

FUN FACT!

The word "space" describes the universe outside of Earth's atmosphere. The universe is always **expanding**.

SUNNY STANDUP

Why didn't the sun need to go to school?

IT ALREADY HAD A MILLION DEGREES.

Where does Earth go on vacation?

IT TAKES A YEARLY TRIP AROUND THE SUN.

Why did the moon break up with the sun?

BECAUSE HE WOULDN'T GO OUT AT NIGHT.

What does the sun drink out of?

SUNGLASSES.

FUN FACT!

Our sun is 93 million miles (149 million km) away from Earth! Light from the sun takes about 8 minutes to reach us.

PLANET PUNCHLINES

What did Jupiter say to Saturn?

"GIVE ME A RING!"

What did Earth say to Venus?

"YOU HAVE NO LIFE."

How does Jupiter hold up its pants?

WITH AN ASTEROID BELT.

What's a planet's favorite kind of music?

NEP-TUNES.

FUN FACT!

In an asteroid belt, a group of asteroids **orbit** the sun together. The main asteroid belt is between Mars and Jupiter.

MOON MATTERS

How does the moon cut his hair?

ECLIPSE IT.

When can't you book a hotel room on the moon?

WHEN IT'S FULL.

Did you hear about the kid who was scared of the moon?

IT WAS JUST A PHASE.

What do you do when you get tired of looking at the moon?

YOU CALL IT A DAY.

FUN FACT!

The moon has different phases, which it cycles through each month. It changes from new moon to full moon, and then goes back again.

GRAVITY GOOFS

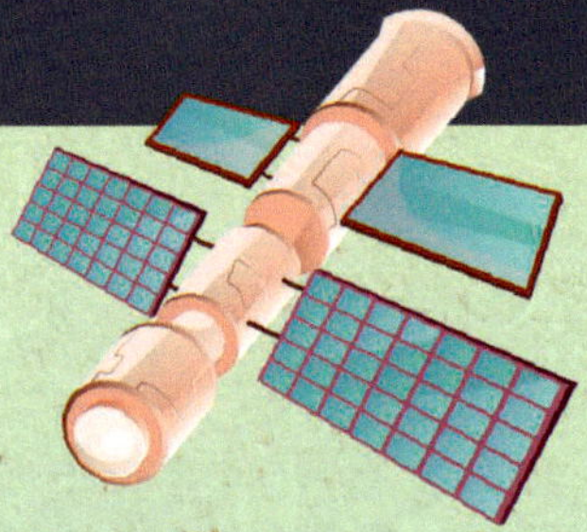

Why is gravity great at organizing events?

IT PULLS EVERYONE TOGETHER!

Have you read the new anti-gravity book?

YES, I COULDN'T PUT IT DOWN!

What kind of drink do astronauts enjoy in space?

GRAVI-TEA.

Why don't aliens take anything seriously?

THEY DON'T UNDERSTAND THE GRAVITY OF THE SITUATION.

FUN FACT!

There's less gravity on the moon than on Earth, so astronauts hop a bit while walking.

AWESOME ASTRONAUTS

How do astronauts put a baby to sleep?

THEY ROCKET.

Why wasn't the astronaut hungry?

SHE JUST HAD LAUNCH.

What do you call an almond in space?

AN ASTRO-NUT.

Where do astronauts park their space shuttles?

NEXT TO THE PARKING METEOR.

FUN FACT!

Astronauts train at NASA's Johnson Space Center in Houston, Texas.

SILLY STARS

Why did the star go to college?

TO GET BRIGHTER!

How do constellations apologize?

THEY SAY "I'M STARRY."

What is money called in space?

STAR BUCKS.

One star says, "I'm the brightest star in the sky!"

THE OTHER SAYS, "YOU CAN'T BE SIRIUS!"

FUN FACT!

Sirius is the brightest star in Earth's sky each night.

GALAXY GIGGLES

What's a cow's favorite galaxy?

THE MILKY WAY.

What body of water is in space?

THE GALAX-SEA.

What did one galaxy say to the other?

"YOU'RE OUT OF THIS WORLD!"

Where do galaxies go to school?

UNIVERSE-ITY.

FUN FACT!

Earth is in the Milky Way galaxy. Our galaxy is about 100,000 light years across. That means it would take light 100,000 years to get from one end to the other!

ALIEN ANTICS

What did the alien wear to his wedding?

A SPACE SUIT.

What should you do if you make an alien angry?

GIVE HIM SOME SPACE.

What's an alien's favorite food?

UNIDENTIFIED FRYING OBJECTS.

Why don't aliens visit Earth?

THEY'VE SEEN THE REVIEWS—IT HAS ONLY ONE STAR.

FUN FACT!

Unidentified flying objects (UFOs) haven't been found to belong to aliens. UFOs are usually meteors, the space station, military planes, or other space objects.

GLOSSARY

asteroid: A small, rocky body in space.

atmosphere: The gases surrounding Earth or other similar objects in space.

constellation: A group of stars in the sky that is thought to look like, and is named after, an animal, object, or person.

eclipse: The blocking from view of the sun, a moon, or a planet by another body in space.

expand: To become bigger.

gravity: The force that pulls objects toward a body in space.

launch: To send into the air with great force.

meteor: A bright streak or flash in the sky that happens when pieces of space material enter Earth's atmosphere and burn up.

orbit: A path in which a body in space moves in a circle around another body.

phase: A stage in a process or sequence of events.

unidentified: Not identified, or named.

FOR MORE INFORMATION

BOOKS

Gardner, Jane P. *Constellations.* Minneapolis, MN: Jump!, 2021.

Stott, Carole. *Planets.* New York, NY: DK Publishing, 2023.

Tolli, Jenna. *Astronaut.* Buffalo, NY: PowerKids Press, 2025.

WEBSITES

Stars
www.ducksters.com/science/star.php
Discover super facts about stars, and follow their life cycle.

What Is a Planet?
kids.nationalgeographic.com/space/article/what-is-a-planet
Learn more about planets with National Geographic Kids.

INDEX